Bird Writer's
Handbook

Bird Writer's Handbook

Allan Safarik

TORONTO

Exile Editions
2002

This edition is published by Exile Editions Limited,
20 Dale Avenue, Toronto, Ontario, Canada   M4W 1K4

Sales Distribution:
McArthur & Company
c/o Harper Collins
1995 Markham Road
Toronto, ON
M1B 5M8
toll free:
1 800 387 0117
(fax) 1 800 668 5788

Design & Composition by TIM HANNA
Cover Design by ZERO WEATHER
Typeset at MOONS OF JUPITER INC.
Printed and Bound at TRANSCONTINENTAL PRINTING

The publisher wishes to acknowledge
the assistance toward publication of
the Canada Council and the Ontario Arts Council.

THE CANADA COUNCIL | LE CONSEIL DES ARTS
FOR THE ARTS | DU CANADA
SINCE 1957 | DEPUIS 1957

ONTARIO ARTS COUNCIL
CONSEIL DES ARTS DE L'ONTARIO

ISBN 1-55096-568-9

for
Kathleen Mabel Safarik

Contents

Selected Translations
from *Okira*

Mt. Hira / 13
Cormorant / 14
Swallows in the Rafters / 15
The Horse Is Loose in the Mountain Pasture / 16
Again and Again from My Sickbed I Ask / 20

Do Birds Live
in a Blue World?

Icarus / 25
The Other Side as Things Pass On / 26
Spinnaker / 28
Semiahmoo Bay 30
Trap / 31
Pitt River Road / 32
Tokens from the Heart / 33
Do Birds Live in a Blue World? / 34
Almost an Epigram / 36
The Definition of Our Love / 37
The Bird / 38
Winter Sun / 39
When Hummingbirds Pollinate the Cows / 40
Rock River Poem / 42
The Owl / 43
The Logic Trick / 44
Saskatoon / 45
Red Parrots in the Blue Jungle / 46
Yellow Bird / 47
Mimicry of Birds at War / 48

Mexican Winter / 49
Near the End of the Moment / 50
The Cage / 52

Black Swans

Shooting Gallery / 57
Black Swans / 58
Unreasonable Doubt / 59
The Attic / 60
The Patient / 62
Fish Candy / 64
Octopus / 66
Herring Gull / 68
Victory Square / 70
Poetry Bird / 71
Grace Street / 72
Laughing in the Rain / 74

Far Field

White Birds / 79
North Kamloops / 80
Medicine Hat / 81
Flickers / 82
Far Field / 83
Swainson's Hawk / 84
Edge / 85
Magpie Song / 86
Bird of Prey / 88
Final Instructions / 89
Memory of the Sky / 90
Advice to a Young Dog / 91
Heat Wave / 92

Dream Without Water / 93
The Fire / 94
Weather Vane / 95
Marshland / 97
Wild Turkey / 99
Death You Say Is on Your Mind / 100
Dog Tail / 101
Draft Horses / 103
Poultry / 104
White Leghorns at Christmas / 106
Magpie Winter / 107
Winter Road / 108

Witness

Blood of Angels / 113
From Holy Ladder / 115
Martyrs / 116
The Dog's Black Lips / 117
Probable Scenario / 118
God's Breakfast Food / 120
Into the Forest / 121
Meditation on a Bird's Skull / 122
Meeting the Apostles on the Road to Heaven / 123
The Grave / 124
Magician / 125
Like Napoleon Leaving Russia / 126
Siege / 128
Meditations on an Empty Pail / 129
Witness / 130
Winter Epilogue / 131
Hymn for the Last One Left on Earth / 132

Notes / 135

Selected Translations
from *Okira*

MT. HIRA

September morning, I trim my brushes and
prepare the ink. The mist since dawn is
smoke from some distant fire. In green
spring the gulls come west from the sea
to rob the songbirds of their tender young.
The crows and gulls are clear and loud above
the trees. I am glad of the mist to hide
the killing from my sad eyes. The songbirds
my friends, wake me and remind me to light
the lamp. In return I paint them and have
them near even in winter when the trees are
bare and the snow drifts half-way to the eaves.

A hunter passing my shanty beside the path
has a monkey slung from his shoulder. The
arrow trimmed with white and blue feathers
still imbedded in the soft wet body. I put
wood on the fire and listen to his singing
long after he has disappeared into the mist.
In the afternoon washing my clothes on the
smooth stones in the icy creek I stop before
the trail of fresh blood on the spent leaves

13

CORMORANT

the fisherman
has taken on
the countenance
of the bird

the man, the bird, the man
one is a beggar without the other

no matter
it is all
the same
fish

SWALLOWS IN THE RAFTERS

swallows
year by year
build
mud nest
in the rafters
of my drafty hut

in spring
I am so relieved
when first I see
the swallows

THE HORSE IS LOOSE
IN THE MOUNTAIN PASTURE
I COULDN'T HOBBLE HIM FOR LIFE

(by Ojibe Kurome, wife of the guard Kurashashibe
Aramushi, trans. from Okira)

I

the mountain is a grey horse
running through the stream
into the meadow of wild hay

the geese in the lake end
lift off on the sorrow
of a thousand black wings

the cold hawk distant as the heavens
is hidden by his own stray flight

the old woodcutter of Kitsu
returns home full of saki
leaving his red sash on the trail

II

the willow
wears
a beard
of frost

the crow
on the fence
post
is black
as the fire
stick

at morning
the hands
binding hair
are white
as rice cakes

III

the smoky lamp barely flickers
in this the third moon of fall
the shanty roof keeps out the stars
burning in the clear night sky
the Dog Star howls at the silver moon
the ducks in their bamboo pen grow restless

IV

from Hira
carrying home
on our backs
sacks of buckwheat
"the flowers of frost"

at camp
on the mountain
in the pines
eating trout
and red berries
gathered
near the stream

cooking
the fish
on green
sticks
above
the comforting
heat of white-
hot rock

at evening
the crane
from hiding
flew
into the pale
moon

V

North
from this place through
the Five Gates of Stone
is a world of trouble
the yellow curs on the road
are thin and sickly
the children are invisible
with the women
the rice paddies are dry
and deserted
this birthplace is better
forgotten
there are more graves
than men.

AGAIN AND AGAIN
FROM MY SICKBED I ASK
HOW DEEP IS THE SNOW?

(Masaoka Shiki)

This northern cold has no respect for walls
In winter I am at the end of the road at the
corner of the world. How deep is the snow?

Every day I write 100 haikus
about the wind and
snow

Soon to die
I am noisier than ever
I am the bird that has
forgotten to leave

At my side there is no soft voice to whisper
"How dear to me you are." I have only the
grave and the snow and a son far away.

How deep is the snow?

There is ice in the tree-
limbs the stream is silent
frozen till spring
warms my numb feet

Every season is so different
Yet the moon goes on
shining
with the same light

The birds
that I painted in my youth
give comfort
but I cannot claim the unreal
as real

How deep is the snow?

Even the candle has a cold blue flame
that drips tears without passion

Each night I hear the horse crossing
the ice. Hear the dull thud of dead
memories crossing the ice. Hear the
huge cracks spreading in the black ice
Hear myself saying: How deep is the snow?

Do Birds Live
in a Blue World?

ICARUS

I

the moulting robin
fat
ragged
on the fence post

II

flying-up
a ripe berry
hanging in the sky

III

a flame
in the green tree

THE OTHER SIDE AS THINGS PASS ON

Eye of the bird
Song of the soul's open window
A spent flower is sweet spit
in the wind
A child's drawing of himself
is how he thinks he appears to others
A man's drawing of himself
is how he wishes to appear to others
In the slow night of the sleeping cactus
the flower comes but once a year
It is a hook through the air
to the other side
It is the irresistible diadem
in a lifetime
That plant that hasn't budged so long
shows its colour, its hour of joy
for the cycle
It is an entrance and an exit
Both things an admission of the living.
Think of the chemical power
Today a hummingbird
hovered before the kitchen window
The only hummingbird of summer
on the last day of summer.
Its beauty is a tragedy so sublime
There is no end to it,
Think of the energy
A snake with a red line,

26

Bright as the running sign
of the razor
Thin red smile on snakemeat
Taking sun on pavement
Cars whiz by

SPINNAKER

by ocean the trees
are rags

shreds of themselves
always dipping to the sea

the spirit bows

arbutus with its orange
scarred bark

is crippled and blind

but will not give in

will grow from a dark
thin crack

will move the rock
in time

is patient
and hard growing

under a bleached moon
and the roar of surf

through blank months
of west coast rain

and the withered mornings
of listless constant mist

the sea's same old face
upturned to the sky

open and moving
open and moving

in the branches
in perfect balance

a small but brilliant bird
wind tugging his coat

is ripping discord

SEMIAHMOO BAY

Crows, seagulls, rats
scavengers of the beach
Then there is the white
two-legged thing, upright
that bares its back, legs
sloped shoulders to the sea

He feeds them all garbage
to raise the giant fan of wings
a flapping greedy circus
the pleasures of his body
baking under tinted glasses

I see him beneath the waves
swimming bird-like in fish skin
lovely fluttering butterfly bait
cold fear might turn to stone
sinking far down into water darkness

The gleaners of the deep wait below
where crabs are crows in armour
beaks are claws brain is hunger
eyes are stars in silver dollar lives
Surreal trees, soft green strangling
ropes wind around arms, stripped torso

The halibut white belly
signals mayhem and the feast
Pail of blood dumped into the sea
The stormy sands polish, grind bone
necklace for the worshipping tides
that rise to moon and sun

TRAP

Here gunshots are scarce
as the dead pigeon
I found in the alley
stuffed into a Kleenex box,
shot through the breast

In California somebody
is chopping the bills
from living pelicans
with tin snips or a hatchet
And gunshots are about
as frequent as heart attacks

The smart ones
tape a handgun into the back
of the toilet

PITT RIVER ROAD

On the wire
clumps of ice
mistaken for birds

the man with frozen hands
repairing his car
early morning
side-of-the-road
surrounded
by desolate fields
of paper corn
and a hedgerow
of hazel trees

Look again
and you'll see
those birds
were real enough
disguised as ice

TOKENS FROM THE HEART

The robins
in winter
look foolish
in the snow

The cat knows
(claws out like ice)
all about song
birds

I put him out
purring
into the dark
night

DO BIRDS LIVE IN A BLUE WORLD?

(a child asks) *for Jeremy & Jevon*

No, theirs is red and green
Eyes that prick from high
In a cold cross current
of wind that drifts like water
And has a silver side

Eyes that see inside the world
from outside its skin
With a fine penetrating glance
define moving things as quick
as a dog smells his dinner

Birds have feathers carefully muted
as snow. That grow on their bodies
like leaves. Each feather is a charm
different from the next

But birds bruise easily
and die quickly from shock.
They are made to fly

And when they can't they hide
still in a secret spot
Calling to the air. Soon
they are quiet and lost

Birds have a green and red world
because when the frost saws
into the grass

Their tiny hearts encased
in a miracle hollow of bones
tick like fine jewelled watches

And they fly far away

ALMOST AN EPIGRAM

I was taken into the light
by an immaculate bird
It shook its feathered
coat of flames
in the morning sky

Everywhere the sun
evaporated in the grass
Careless as a lover
I saw the bird of summer
waking in your hair

THE DEFINITION OF OUR LOVE

Wounded, small and grey
with a leaking hole
in its pigeon breast
It flies around the room
bumping furniture
thumping into windows

like a padded fist

THE BIRD

there is strength in gentleness
take the bird soaring above his life
green trees below waking in the sun
wind disturbing quiet water
air rushing through his sieve of feathers
like your mouth where everything
returns to take on pleasure
the beautiful wings of your hands
nailed to the gauntlet of your wrists
I hunger for you around the blueness
of the wide open earth

there is strength in gentleness
I would soar for you
if these flapping hands of mine could fly
many nights I went down trying
lost in the mountains of my desire
in the morning when everything whole
was chained in the impossible light
your wings spread into the heat
of the luminous summer's day
and you disappeared in the unreturning sky
leaving me here nailed to my clumsy feet

WINTER SUN

A few miserable sparrows
hop among the barren grape vines
I put the cage of my hand around
the winter sun. The birds leave it empty
The cat hiding in the restless leaves
gnaws happily on a mole's pink head
Fat little mole body chugging away
like a breast-stroking engine

Death is perfunctory to the domesticate
The well-fed cat extracts the gruesome
toll of cruelty and mutilation
with an innocent flicking tail

Nature is perfect in desire!
I catch nothing but the cold light
in the cage of my hand
Bring it in, warm it by the fire

WHEN HUMMINGBIRDS POLLINATE THE COWS

A hummingbird, bluey-green
flare in the mist of the morning—
hovers over fields wet with dew
Blurred wings fanning manure-stained haunches
A helicopter circles flapping tails
the handles on the slippery udders
moving accurately as clockwork
around the acres of chloroform
The hummingbird dips
into each and every bovine
with his needle bill
with purple sheen
with ruby throat
with iridescent slashes
with summer in the meadow of buttercups
The hummingbird trembling
like the voice of flames
enters the plodding beast
on a single strand of light
Beautiful flower sperm
spilling from hummingbird lips
The sun's feathered vessel
darting in and out
whispers of pure adulterated sex
linger here and there
driving them mad with teasing penetration
Farmers will tell you cows can smile
and these cows were smiling
in a landscape wildly gyrating
with tons of cow thighs
thunder-clapping in the clover

40

When hummingbirds pollinate the cows
the sun gawks overhead like a voyeur
through the canopy of blushing trees
crushed plants applaud
with bent stamens, flattened leaves
Grasshoppers whip off green-shelled cod pieces
Silly white ducks with orangy
goose bills play trombone necks
in a horny quacking orchestration
Strutting roosters go mad with anticipation
shaking their sun-shattered tail feathers
across the barnyard like maracas
Even the dragonflies stop
their dull head-snapping
to watch the parabola of bird
humping twelve hundred pound cows
Entering them all quickly a second,
third, and fourth time
His insatiable metabolism
burning in the air/light
Artificial and vaporous
as a rainbow arching in the sky

ROCK RIVER POEM

Lightning bugs
ignite in the
tender night

Big yellow carp
swarm after
mallard ducklings

THE OWL

People think the owl wise
because he looks remarkably similar
to the house cat, who is no dummy
and because he is endowed
with all the tools of the judge

In truth the Chinese call owl
the cat bird and though he eats
the same little mammals as cat
and has sharp feline ears
he is not very bright

But don't pity the owl
when the songbirds find him
roosting in the daytime
the invective and hatred he endures
would make a wiser creature paranoid

Not the owl, his reversal is
swooping in pillow-dark madness
No time for pleas or emotion
he sentences each rodent impartially
with his legal beak, judicial talons

43

THE LOGIC TRICK

Blue iridescent turtle
walks along the highway
Sun on his back
sour in the shell
Gulls appear
in the desert

SASKATOON

this European river
passing like vodka
under black iron bridges
sweet green city
on the Danube, the Volga

the magpies here
are wiser than dust
with their witty glass eyes
and ballroom suits—
drunk all the time!

Maybe old people die
and turn into magpies
the one in the elm tree
telling me a tragic story
about her useless daughter

RED PARROTS IN THE BLUE JUNGLE

Of wounding teeth
there are plenty of stories

The dental deformities
which caused certain Bengal tigers
to become man-eating Gods
stripping and devouring
blood-soaked clothes

Septic holes pouring forth
from the mauled victims
(who were almost always
carried off alive)
filling up with cries
of tropical birds,
coughing deer

Of your wounding teeth
grazing like small hatchets
on the pastures of my throat
And my larger jungle ones
following your outline
down the hills
of darkness

YELLOW BIRD

Urgent yellow bird
species unidentified
beating fancy scarves
around the breeze

something damaged
makes the flapping
a pitiful banner
cries reach the street

Striped cat rushes in
and away with lemon feathers
bouquet of strange flowers
boasting in its jaws

fluttering tail
pinions broken
neck an awkward question mark
bird returned like lost property

47

Does this quickly
disappearing drama
have the confidence
of the landscape?

beak opening, closing
with a metallic snap
black eye
pointed at the sky

MIMICRY OF BIRDS AT WAR

I found these words, assembled them in space
The machine moves along the line
with authority, making
important black marks
A blank field fills with ideas
All of them untried and unregistered
A sudden movement, everything spills
back into the pool of chance
Pages fall still on the floor

The secondary message could not
be verbally translated
Birds on the wires speaking
through the voice of nests
repeated transpacific telephone calls
There was a great deal of repetition
and mass regurgitations
In the morning, white fields
illustrated calligraphy of crows

MEXICAN WINTER

Parrots frozen
to the palm trees
dust has the sting of ice
beer bottles thawed
with a blowtorch
bugs all die in a day
nothing moving but de-
iced wings of an impaired
fly stuck on the sun-
burned window

Fat water-logged jungle
shatters at the touch
or impulse of the threat
one enraged dog racing
after its tail destroys an acre
of grapefruit trees
glass banana stalks
swept up in a dustpan
chickens in the henhouse
bloat on solid yolks

They are playing road hockey in Oaxaca
ice skating on the lagoons
in the mountains pot growers
harvest purple buds
bird hunters fill sacks
they found a frozen snake
curled around a frozen rat
in a hospital pipe
there are angels visible
above a dozen church spires

49

NEAR THE END OF THE MOMENT

This crow comes to talk
at my early morning window
telling weird stories
about people in the neighbourhood
He loves being raucous and profane
I yell back when he threatens
blackmail, occasionally vow
to take a potshot

The seagulls walking on the roof
in rubber boots, catching up
with the gossip, stay out of it
When the wind is up
they have flying contests
On hot days they go to the pier
and perform aerobatics
for junk food

When you talk a lot to birds
you have to learn to keep
your mind on the quirky eye
I get news of you
inadvertently from strangers
Crow digests it for meaning
No use being desirous of shiny
things or polishing hope
when there isn't

I knew he was lying
When he bragged that he stopped
searching for bright objects
because it leads to trouble
there he was sneaking over the trees
in his usual ambling style
your silver bracelet
in his beak

THE CAGE

the opening in the cage
is not larger than a fist
a hand pushed through
could see light

do you ever feel threatened
by everything in the past?
why the cage left the bird open?
why or where the bird flew?

Black Swans

SHOOTING GALLERY

Shooting our Daisy BB gun
at Graham crackers or the
flames on birthday candles
held by clothes pegs
against the basement wall
Looking through the peep sight
at shadowy flickering targets
my brother and me arguing
under the furnace pipes
about who had the most hits

Mother came down and broke up
the fist fight, confiscating
our newly cocked weapon
Took it upstairs and while
trying to unload it, pulled
the trigger, firing a BB
through the front room window
killing a robin in the hedge

We waited under the stairs
thinking about the tiny round hole
the long jagged crack in the view
of North Shore mountains
until the old man came home from work
Bury that damn bird, is all he said
We did, in a shoe box under the plum tree

BLACK SWANS

Some things never break down
from the rays of the sun
A black car stares
out from a driveway
It's worn down like an old smile
The sun has been working
on it for half a century
Absorbing the shimmering
metallic finish
crushing the fenders
with the weight of light

The nuns from Seton Academy
playing baseball on the field
beside the reservoir
could hit and field
They ran at the crack of the bat
Slid headfirst into second base
We called them the black swans
as they whipped the ball
around the infield

The sun beat them senseless
in their long robes
They withered soon enough
Dust crept over the diamond
fading the black from their lives
They gathered in the shade of the trees
for a cool drink of water
dabbing it on their foreheads
Graceful as swans
We never saw their necks uncovered

UNREASONABLE DOUBT

Every Saturday morning for thirty years
a little brown car pulled up
in front of the house
My mother bought magazines
from Jehovah Witnesses
Awake and *Watchtower*
fit perfectly into the
bottom of the bird cage

She handed them twenty cents
for two stapled magazines
The dog starting barking
when they brought up
spiritual matters
Snapping at persistence
Mother closed the door firmly
on unnecessary conversations

She didn't want to disappoint
anybody working for God
The bird was happy enough
with a clean new bedspread
When he heard their knock
Beating his head incessantly
against the shiny bell

59

THE ATTIC

After midnight in the old house
Fat black cat thumping
on the staircase
Grandpa's snoring
buzzes through the ceiling
Constant creaking in the walls
interrupted by clock chimes

Sudden alarm from the fire hall
Two trucks roar down Penticton Street
A car door slams the dark
Chinese voices converse in the lane
Neighbours home from the restaurant
They'll be gone back to work
again before I wake

Grandma gets up in her room
I turn out the bedside light
until the toilet flushes
She puts out the cat
scolding her in Czech
about bringing home birds
before going back to bed

Pale moonlight in an attic window
Seated at the treadle sewing machine
looking through a pile of tintype photos
legal documents in foreign languages
Many ribbons and wax seals
A box of ancient fountain pens
Bone and tortoise shell

Soft cooing from pigeons
roosting on rooftops
spread the murmur of sleep
I fall into feathers
Soothing sounds of boxcars
shunting on the waterfront
Foghorns in the harbour

THE PATIENT

He had slight grey hands
that covered his mouth
when he coughed

They were the size
of small pigeons
roosting in the sheets
When he talked
they flew around the room
I wanted them to find
a place to land
They wouldn't stop
struggling against
the window's glass

The nurse came in
telling him it was time
for his prep

He walked me to the elevator
in his bathrobe, left me
laughing with a story
about the old neighbourhood
I knew by his eyes,
the colour of sand,
he was preparing to depart

"Don't worry if things
don't work out
I'll send you a message
from the other side"
When I shook his hand
I felt the bird in it
pecking at my palm

Wondering about the pigeons
dangling on his wrists
If I would see them in the sky

FISH CANDY

Stripped cod skeletons
twisted heads and tails
glassy eyes stare at soft dreams
Not a cloud in the blue sky
A barrel of undressed fish
show translucent bones
in the soft Pacific light
A man in a crumpled overcoat
wine stains and a toothless grin
stops by and digs his penknife
into the heads dislodging eyeballs
tosses them into the air
catches each one in his mouth
with a loud sucking sound

A herring gull on the rooftop
swooping down misses the airborne
eyeball and pecks the man hard
in the middle of his face
leaving a brighter red spot than
on the forehead of an East Indian wife
Later he's trying to explain
how it happened to some dock workers
But the sun was too hot and big
drops of blood fell silently
from the hole in his head
When the cops asked who hit him
he muttered about a feed of fish candy
and being mugged by a big bird

When he left in the police car
the bird on the roof was laughing
at him while he banged on the window
On the ride up to Main Street
he was warned not to bleed on the seats
Nurse said stitches wouldn't improve him
More like a beer bottle than a bird
the judge said sentencing him
to ten days for being drunk
and disorderly in a public place
but gave him credit for the story
Fish candy and a big bird is all
he said when he went to jail
They understood completely

OCTOPUS

The octopus
escapes
the fish plant
by forcing
its own matter
for several days
through a drain
pipe

Comes up
onto the land
throwing spears
wrapping the cups
on his arms
around the sun-lit
friction of air

Birds flash
down at him
a blizzard
of yellow feet
slashing bills
wrung necks

Smarter than
a city dog
brain-testicle
hiding in the
scrotum purple
discoloured skin

Plastic eyes
quivering
in the tortured
ease of living
minus bones

HERRING GULL

Plucked it resembles an old boot
Skinny, rubbery fleshed, oily,
raw boned, unappetizing
Looks like a starved
chicken with a complex
Add feathers and you've built
the perfect flying garbage can
carrying an unzippering beak more
useful than a Swiss Army Knife

In city parks they last for years
even when some urban
thrill seeker with a long bow
has shot an arrow through
the body, the bird wanders
over the grass in the rain
dragging the shaft while
picking up bountiful worms

68

Today the seagull's walking
around with a rat caught
in its throat, hind end
hanging out the gaping beak
First the back legs are running
full blast but soon they
slow down until they kick
unconsciously once or twice
every few minutes like
a bad case of the hiccups

The bird stands in the drizzle
for two hours trying to swallow
through an engorged neck
until the head of rat disintegrates
in vile digestive juices
Only the tail dangles down
between sick-looking eyeballs

Finally, the gull lifts off and flies
sideways over the harbour
defecating great white strings
onto the green waves

VICTORY SQUARE

A place to pass the day on green park benches
feeding pigeons or sleeping casually on the grass
One shoe off, head under a thin sheet of newsprint
Claw hand clutching a bottle in a paper bag
Sky thrown over him like a dirty grey blanket
Across the street at Pappas Furs another
full-length silver fox coat gets into a limo
I'm reading my book waiting for the bus

You bastard a voice yelled three times
from behind a pink fluorescent rhododendron
half as big as a boxcar, covered in bloom
I looked around the damp green square
spotted a fierce red face peering
at me from behind the profusion of blossoms
Crows dropping walnuts on the sidewalk
made that sound of rusty hinges on an iron gate

He ceased speaking and moved quickly
pushing into view through the stiff wet branches
A man with the posture and personality of a troll
in a wet raincoat waving a long thin blade
Too late for words, heavy rain began to pelt the leaves

Wind blew ruined flowers against the wire fence
The bus came, I jumped on without delay
Looked back through the rear window
Black knife handle plunging again and again
into the purple darkness of the bushes

POETRY BIRD

In memory of Milton Acorn

Thwack thwack thwack smith corona portable
thumping among the hours with smudgy words
pages float around in a white field of sleep
Milton has written two bird poems in eight hours
The window's glass repeats the image
strange baleful glint in a crazy red-rimmed eye
wandering the room like a lost soldier
cigar melting frost on the morning pane
fat chunks of ash on the sill crumble
to dust under the grey bruising of his thumb
Acrid clouds of his puffing and the sour odour
of socks under the peeling apartment ceiling

His impatience pounces like a stupefied cat
after the quick flighted poetry bird makes
a desperate rush for wide open spaces
but bounces off the glass patio doors
and falls fluttering behind the couch
He fetches it gingerly in his meaty hands
stroking the wings with his knuckles
Tears chuckle down his ruddy cheeks
as he adjusts the struggling bird
back into the typewriter carriage

Thwack thwack the veins in his nose
explode into handfuls of blotchy rose petals
the blood-flowering poetry tree
grows from his chapped face
double-imaged bird in his bulging eyes

GRACE STREET

for John Newlove

Three nights of snow whisper
Through blue attic windows

One skinny light bulb
Hangs in the shadow
Of its own elongated,
Slightly twisted
Chicken-neck cord

Beacon for angels

Undressed night
Moves into a warm room

Above formal wrought-iron fences
And Italian cement lions

A solitary light
Waits the coming
Of the insipid brown moth

Truth needs inquisitors
Like summer needs Sundays

In the midnight garden
Of atrocious wallpaper
A solitary light
Gives off the sun

The dangling man
Dangles in his underwear
In a rooftop street
Afraid this might be
All there is to heaven

A white sandblasted room
A dump truck filled
With rosary beads
One thin coat passing
A prayer from the cold
Through a single blue attic window

Snowfall of souls
Bag of chicken feathers
Drifting in from Grace Street

LAUGHING IN THE RAIN

The bird says *Hello, you got change for the parking meter?*
Caw caw caw chasing me across the street
with his annoying, inane comments
swooping at my stupid army & navy hat
Caw caw caw cheap cheap cheap
Crow is trying to con me into giving him
the Vietnamese take-out salad rolls
I'm eating boldly in front of his beady-eyed beak
Finally, in a gesture to restore harmony in the neighbourhood
like scattering a handful of marigold seeds in the universe
I give him a piece of my last salad roll
In the alley of alleged cobblestone atrocities, behind the cop shop
Crow asks *Want to buy a set of used dentures?*
Probably beaten out of some poor old wino's head
Caw caw caw snap snap snap
Teeth without a mouth chewing on the gusting wind
Crow deals in prophecies and petty games of chance
I watch him rolling a small silver fish head around in the gutter
When Crow's around, things on the wire drop dead
the black rain of sparrows fills up the gutters
neon in Chinatown begins to sputter in the rain
trolley buses on Hastings Street stop running

Crow sent Tom and me into the time capsule, Room 412
the Arlington Hotel, twentieth-century skid row dive
to meet Crow's friend, Crazy Eyes, the doll collector from out-of-town
Wild blue pools of sight, boiled like twin cyclones
in the gaunt, unshaven, ravine-scarred-face of the junkie angel
on semi-permanent vacation in a downtown east side location
He wants badly to sell his collection for quick cash
When he opened the closet door a thousand sock monkeys
fell on the floor

On our way out the desk clerk said he was wanted in Quebec
Wanted for bad taste, black velvet Venus and a bare light bulb
or the tattoo of his mother's heart on the fleshy part of his arm

In the morning Crow touches the blue graffiti from
the black squalling night before
strutting through rush hour traffic like a drum major on his day off
small dead mammals are Crow's buffalo; the city his convenience store
If you talk back to Crow he'll answer in fifty languages
In two minutes your head will fall off,
he'll be living in style inside your hat
and you'll be paying him the rent on time
He's on the ground now hopping around the garbage bin
smooth slick sheen of smeared Vaseline glistening in the rain
caw caw caw move your dumbassed car
caw caw caw I want the McDonald's bag
caw caw caw under the rear wheel

Far Field

WHITE BIRDS

Left the coast at daybreak
Watched white birds veering out
over the bay disappear in the fog
covering the view of islands
obscuring corrugated water

I was drowning looking at water
Couldn't find appropriate words
to master changes in the weather
Silence is a stone weapon
No sound exists to stop it for long

Passing one last time in fall
through shadowy mountains
New snow on the glacier
bright pile of feathers
between granite peaks
Blue walls rise into the sun

Nothing restless about mountains
Light leaves quickly pausing
at the edges of jagged rock
Finding a dislocated soul
in a small pocket of time
Darkness comes slamming down

NORTH KAMLOOPS

The blind man in the thrift store
knocked over a bird cage
and a table full of china tea cups
The dirty white kitten landed
in a pile of plastic dishes

I bought a sports jacket for five bucks
When I got back to the motel
and tried it on again it didn't fit
It was too short in the sleeves
The street smelled of KFC chicken

When I took it back the woman said
I could leave it on consignment
or take something in trade
I was too freaked out by the smell of death
wafting down from the big ceiling fan

The cat stretched out in the window
An old-fashioned wrap
for an old woman's pitiful neck
"Did he buy all those broken saucers?"
"Lucky there was no bird to go missing."

MEDICINE HAT

It was so hot the sun was making
big fingerprints in the street
Outside town, in the dust
a grasshopper army was munching alfalfa
Three red-tailed hawks sat
preening on the fenceline
Even the air force was grounded

We travelled miles through a cloud of wings
Insect cockpits shattering on the windshield
When we came out the other side
seagulls were leaving a freshly
ploughed fallow field
lifting off like helium balloons

Faces in the gas station café
had dry prairie smiles
and weather forecasts in the eyes
Car tires were like soft licorice
The smell said the radiator
was about to go on the boil

We waited, drinking coffee
until darkness came around again
Suddenly we had no headlights
I asked the attendant if he fixed shorts
"No I pump gas and make coffee"
Drove all night by moonlight
through the gallery of shooting stars

FLICKERS

They make a noise
like an electrical discharge
when they arrive
to patrol the lawn
Standing erect
sharp pointed heads
tilt at the sky

They have a peculiar habit
of remaining aloof
as if looking for trouble
that doesn't exist
hopping awkwardly around
gyrating in circles
suddenly stopping to listen

The bird woman said:
"No you haven't got it right
Flickers are more sophisticated
than you think
They pause to overhear
bugs in conversation
before they dine"

I declined asking her
the significance
of the bright red moustache
for fear she would tell me
it was in honour of Groucho Marx
or some weird decoration
awarded by Audubon

FAR FIELD

The plough breaks up the earth
white birds dipping behind
clouds of wings, frenzied cries

I watch the green tractor for hours
moving in the distance to the edge
nearly vanishing on the horizon

It returns dragging a ribbon of dust
The kid says, "Look it's pulling the sky"
In the transformation the birds are lost

SWAINSON'S HAWK

A dot on the blue sky
passing across white clouds
drifts down over the fields
crafting wings around air currents
methodically sweeping the ground
until it sees the gopher's silhouette
caught in a nervous movement
standing upright at its hole

The attitude of wings
in a brief fragment of time
drops talons into the equation
the bird on course at speed
aiming at its paralyzed target
hits it with opened razors
A small explosion of dust
and blood on twisting feathers

EDGE

In a field of broken stones
Things come down from the sky
Hawks before the last light
Shifting in the wind
Above the rattle in the grass

In the closing moments
The sun completes its fade
Behind the picket of willows
Blood leaves the clouds
Stars begin to show

Darkness covers the dust
Everything warm vanishes
For all the things that glitter
Constellations on the dome of the sky
Town lights on a frozen field

The radio brings in country
Music and weird static
A stranger's voice begs for money
Animal eyes stare at headlights
Black wings fly across the moon

85

MAGPIE SONG

Circular saws sing a lovelier song
than the black-and-white whirlwind
building their stick high-rise in my shade tree
I go out and poke it down with a long pole
I keep in the garage for that very purpose
You think it's easy, living in Siberia, Saskatchewan
when the grasshoppers decide your garden's
on the menu or the big borers arrive
to finish the onions off

The birds decide to build higher up
in a crotch beyond my reach
While I wobble on the ladder
trying to get the damn bird jumble down
more mosquitoes than I've ever seen
harvest the blood straight from my veins
I may as well send it to the blood bank in a tin cup
No offence, I know there's nothing personal
about the way nature takes charge
but I'm sweating and fuming
wishing I had a big smelly cigar
so I could puff up a cloud of flack

While thinking about the advantages
of using dynamite in the yard
I notice the air-conditioned neighbours
(afraid to come out of their house
for fear of anaemia)
are watching from their upstairs window
while the birds go round and round
banging their tails in the wind

Although I am ignorant of bird language
I take the shrieking rage as threats of murder
Thinking about all the times I've been driven
out of bed by magpies torturing the dog
I straighten up my bitten ass end
and work vigorously until I knock it out

When the nest came clattering down
around my head and the ladder fell
into the Caragana hedge
I lay in a heat daze from the
massive loss of bodily fluids
Now in the blood prick of my skin
the vocabulary of magpie singing
the Antichrist song of war

BIRD OF PREY

The banker is going
over my cold accounts
like a hungry vulture perched
on a coagulating gopher
"I'm afraid the bank can't..."
Before he finished
I was up shaking his hand
with dead white fingers

Bits of clotted blood,
matted hair, cotton batting
blew out from the hole
in the back of my head
His hunched form defecated
on the glass-topped table

FINAL INSTRUCTIONS

Burn this man
in a plain cardboard box
with a label that says
THIS SIDE UP

Don't leave him too long
with the undertaker

Scatter the ashes
in a friendly place
where birds sing
and children play

MEMORY OF THE SKY

Once my eyes, clean as the moon
in the dark blue night of the summer sky
saw you clearly in the shift of memories
I walked home along the river bank listening
to symphonic frogs croaking in unison
The jarring repetition of an unknown bird
erupted on the thin skin of darkness
I stopped the screams by letting blood
flow out from the crook in my left arm

Let it be known like a broken dream
evaporating in the unrequited dawn—
the white bird lifting off in the mist
flew straight into my shining eyes
I remember the bitter day you left
the brightness of flashing wings
Staying behind, trailing my hands
and feet in watery images of time,
I stare into the heat of the sun

ADVICE TO A YOUNG DOG

Pitying the sound of the neighbour's dog
whining on the front stairs at forty below
I call him over to our house and feed him
all the leftover roast beef from dinner
So grateful, he licks the palm of my hand
Afterward, he curls up under the kitchen table
and falls asleep muttering in dog language
I wonder what's he dreaming about?
Maybe, about putting a cat up the maple tree
the smell of dog urine in the grass
or the decomposed chicken carcass
dragged across the yard

In the summer I watch him watching
magpies from the corner of his clever eye
until they land beside his food dish
Suddenly he rushes at them barking,
shaking his floppy ears, and the sloppy
strings of drool that fly off his jaws
It's not about catching them or the kill
When they fly off in raucous debate
he sits in the shade lolling his tongue,
licking his mouth's red wound before
he lies down panting at the heat
Sad eyes full of blood

HEAT WAVE

Misery loves the company of broken dreams
the way drought slowly ruins a dry land farmer
as if he were an unwatered plant, wilted,
you might say, like an oily rag
In the extreme heat of the afternoon
near cottonwood trees a rusting car craves
the challenge of a panting dog

Scream of hawk travels through shattered glass
into the faded rooms of an abandoned house
In a trailer across the overgrown yard
a wife and child wait patiently for the prisoner
who is never coming home because
of the blood he is spilling this afternoon

At dawn the nervous bird greets the sun, singing
a foolish song, for his delivery from the void
White dust slowly strangling stunted trees

DREAM WITHOUT WATER

In water-starved country
heat distorts the vision
Face and lips are peeling
like an exotic vegetable in hot oil
I stagger forth reaching for the
mirage of dancing water that
bleeds on the edge of the horizon

I fall grovelling in the white sand
dunes among thorny cacti
There's relief in my slow demise
Water or the coolness of a breeze
would have only prolonged the agony
Soon I will dry up like a desiccated bird
caught on the cruel barb in the wire

Not a cloud in the thin blue sky
Ball of the sun frying in the pan
Shadows of circling birds of prey
flicker on sandy waves like wispy
handwriting on corrugated paper
My sunburned soul lingers in the light
balancing between afterworlds

THE FIRE

Everything on earth burning
The crackling trees going up in clouds
of white impenetrable smoke
Ditch grass rips along
the wind in flaming sheets
Clothes on the line smoulder
against the patchy blue sky

The crow on the fence post
already charred and disfigured
with his split tongue cries for pity
but the merciless sun beats down
on his blackened tail feathers
and the curious glass eyes
that shine out from his head

On the top of the hill the houses
start to catch fire, hoses trained
on the shingles cannot stop
the heat from grabbing hold
Inside in my bedroom asleep
I can hear voices in the street yelling
but I never wake up in time

The inferno never stops burning
in the unconscious nights
Smoke breathes through my pillow
The bed levitates on a ledge of fire
In the poem written in the dream
I cry out like the anxious bird
hard glass in my eyes

WEATHER VANE

Sparrows tangled in horse hair
build their nest in the crotch
of chokecherry wood
I wander in the fields
looking for good stones
for medicine dreams
Watch the hawk soaring
against the river of air
He has eyes that see
farther than stars

In a few minutes the sun
drops behind the horizon
bloody sun spreading
in sandy coloured clouds
I walk back beside the garden
smell onions growing
in the black earth
listen to shiny-winged
crows flying around
their roost in a frenzy

Every day a day of wind
but for months,
the spring rain holds off
Thunder heads pass by
rumbling in the distance
Every few seconds another
flash of lightning across
the front of the sky
Cock spinning wildly
on the barn roof

By morning only half
an inch of rain in the glass
the dry wind already
licking it up in a swirling
cloud of dust
Damn bird turning
this way and that way
making a dry thirsty noise
like a rusty gate

MARSHLAND

The long hard winter was over
It all seemed to happen in a day
Snow got dirtier as the months passed by,
suddenly the streets turned into mud
and dead-looking fields
began to show fringes of grass

The pattern of migratory birds
descended from the jet stream
The marshes were alive with pintails,
mallards, blue-winged teal, lesser scaups,
red-winged and yellow-headed blackbirds
A flock of Canada geese settled
in the slough on the edge of town
A long black wave of squawking individuals
pass low overhead, followed by small groups
and the plaintive honking of stragglers
Returning at nighfall
from grazing tender grass shoots
in still desolate grain fields

A kestrel hovers over the marsh effortlessly
adjusting the tilt of wings on a slingshot of air
Bobbing Eurasian coots,
dressed like monks at prayer,
putter around the pothole,
as if on the verge of neurological breakdowns
Swans in the background drift by
silent white puzzle pieces
in a landscape that swallows everything,
including the human eye

In the sandhills, day withers in the bush tops
Copper moon in the cloudless lake of the sky
Somewhere in the distance
a strange bout of coughing
turns into the coyote's call
Meadowlark songs pierce the skin of time
Beautiful throat of God singing about paradise
Red ball of the sun drops a stone
into the mouth of water

WILD TURKEY

Mix-up in the bar
there was nothing to it

a dead man
came in looking
for an old
drinking buddy

found him
in the arms
of his widow

a week later
it happened again
when wind blew
in the back door

the woman
who smells of
cinnamon sticks
was puking
in the corner

the same black
dog had her
by the sleeve

DEATH YOU SAY IS ON YOUR MIND

Well pilgrim, which road were you travelling down?
Not sure, only know it was made of gravel and
the Devil on his day off picked me up hitchhiking
somewhere near Cranberry Flats
In the prairie sky white birds rode the troughs
until gusts whipped them off like pieces of rag

Slow-motion thoughts ticking down
the credits in the movie of my own death
fence posts snap and the wire zings back
against the sound of ripping metal
roll over in a ditch full of tiger lilies
brilliant orange flowers floating in the light

make a halo around the image of the sun
melodic bird songs in the background
hold their electric notes until the static wipes
them out and the next master of song cuts loose
This was the end of time, you might say
the steady green hum of scrubby bush

DOG TAIL

In memory of Smith Atimoyoo

Smith, when you died
birds stopped singing
for a while, water ran
backwards up the creek
the crazy man cut his flesh
on a blade of grass
the storyteller went home
to the medicine woman
Wind blew in buffalo clouds
Desperate men
travelled from afar
and the hobbled old women
who sang the young girl
songs, decades ago, came
home to see you off

At Manito Lake
dappled Indian ponies
vanished in clouds
on the blue horizon
Every place at Little Pine,
eagle shadows fell in the sky
Stones whispered gone
into the muffled wind
ripping at canvas tipi flaps
Stoic elders looking
through curious bird eyes
got up and hopped
around like big ravens
the white woman
with all the pain
found her way to God

Smith, on the day
the badger took Gerald's
advice about risking
a bullet in the head
and decided to walk
away and live, you said
Life begins again
at the end of the journey
under summer clouds
where the river
in the wilderness
turns on the prairie
children play
in the berry bushes

DRAFT HORSES

They stand in the barn contentedly chewing
Tossing huge heads in the shadowy afternoon
A cackling red hen scurries underfoot

One muscle in a monolithic shoulder twitches
A dinner-plate-sized hoof lifts in the air
Comes back down on the floor with a clatter

Putting their heads together like wise men
Great gentle eyes look me over
They seem to stand forever in the silence

POULTRY

The white wind shakes trees
loose of shattering ice
A snowdrift taller
than a school bus
covers the barn door

Nothing in there
but clumps
of dried manure
in empty horse stalls
and the odd white
quirky hen with
her jaunty eye,
perky comb

Everyday she
lays an egg
in a different place.
Early in the morning
she hopped out
onto the roof
making flapping
motions like she
was going to fly

Just before takeoff
an egg clattered
down the shingles
and dropped
into the snow-
bank below

Back inside
she spent her day
pecking at grubs
in the earth floor

WHITE LEGHORNS AT CHRISTMAS

Snow sifting down, shifting by the
angle of the wind. Everything white drifts,
low visibility through the grey bush line
Day after day the sameness continues
Nothing happens for several weeks
until the fox appears beside the chickens

One by one they start disappearing overnight
The others become so traumatized they
forget about the thirty-five below temperature
and start laying eggs like slot machines
on the payout dropping loonies into a tub
when they aren't huddled around the light bulb
or being dragged across the yard
in the jaws of the quick smiling redhead

He ends his nightly sessions by putting
his neck in a wire loop meant for assassins
Frozen to death in a snarling mood
he strangled himself trying to escape
Coyotes tear the stiff body apart
in a few moments of cold gluttony
while the dogs barking in fury
stay close to the yard lights

The chickens are back to barely
surviving the hoar frost, shaking their
combs at the thinness of the light bulb,
Afraid they might lay an ice cube
they cluster together on the perch
barely able to squeeze an ample dropping

MAGPIE WINTER

The hunter's sudden kill
falls in the coulee
Summons Magpies
swishing long tails
through a blizzard
of willow branches
Flying erratic maneuvers
Waiting impatient
the moment of the knife
when dull steaming innards
pulled into light become
discards on bloody ground

Invisible in black-and-white patterns
Waiting for the sound of the shot
against the bottom of the sky
Magpies appear chattering
urgent warnings, swoop down
to steal congealing fat
large quirky eyes, shrill laughter
the price of silence broken
when the hunter drags his game away
Raven croaking a simple death song
hops across the snow
Magpies stunned momentarily
by the vision of pestilence
shout murderous threats
slashing the air with tail fathers
Raven sitting on the gut pile
flares jet-black wings
makes himself bigger
Dipping his head
graciously into the gore

WINTER ROAD

Time moves through memory
An empty road vanishes
into the deserted country
Broken of considering big dreams
the years grow shorter
I counted the number of bones
on the bottom of my feet
Streets are getting tougher
I'm walking on thin ice
wary of every dull sound

Finished the temporary job
Couldn't collect the money
Magazines stopped paying
The last cheque bounced
It's nearly forty below
and Bing Crosby is singing
"White Christmas" on the radio

All day the cold sun
hooked a white knuckle
into the blue sky
Red fox, mange turned
into a grotesque
arrangement of bones
on a roadkill
Big black birds hop
along in his tracks

Wind drifts snow in the desert
Tumbleweed snowmen roll
across stubble fields
Ice crystals sting the air

At the edge of the naked eye
Small black figures gradually
move away along the treeline
Blue snow fills in the shadows
Images remain untouched

Sick fox eating porcupine fat
Birds waiting around for death
Thin light from the sun
White meadows of snow

Witness

BLOOD OF ANGELS

Black-and-white kitty
preening outside
the kitchen door
one opaque eye
in a quizzical face
hairless scars
running the length
of its thin back
as if it escaped
from a skinning
machine
or a maniac with
a filleting knife

Blood-red
underneath white
grey-fringed clouds
evening piling up
in the western sky
sun peering above
the horizon like
a half-cooked egg

I sit down
on the hard bench
put my hand
tentatively
on its head

it purrs, rubbing
against my leg
songs of birds
nesting
in the chimneys
light dying
on the tin roof

FROM HOLY LADDER

When for some reason
I was sitting outside a monastery,
near the cells of those living in solitude,
I heard them fighting by themselves
in their cells like caged partridges
from bitterness and anger,
leaping at the face of their offender
as if he were actually present.

I devoutly advised them
not to stay in solitude in case
they should be changed
from human beings into demons.

One could see how the tongues
of some of them were parched
and hung out of their mouths like a dog's.
Some chastised themselves in the scorching sun,
other tormented themselves in the cold.

Some, having tasted a little water
so as not to die of thirst, stopped drinking;
others, having nibbled a little bread,
flung the rest of it away, and said that
they were unworthy of being fed
like human beings, since they had
behaved like beasts.

– found in the writings of St. John Climacus,
Abbot at the Monastery of Sinai, sixth century

MARTYRS

They grow
in the fields,
upright men
Bright green
arms raised to
the blazing sun

Birds jump
among them
splattering
bloody drops
on straw mulch

When dry
and withered
they are snipped
off close to
the ground

THE DOG'S BLACK LIPS

Growing from rich ground,
the tulip's black petals shine in the light
Rain falls gently in the morning
The wheelbarrow leaves its wheel
mark across the manicured lawn
The gardener's footprints
sluff along behind like brackets
around a piece of printed text

When birds stop singing
darkness creeps over the eyes
Thoughts beautiful as spring
flowers begin to die on mass
Blood in the throat runs cold
flesh turns the colour of ivory
The panting dog's pink tongue
lolling from black lips
announces the arrival of angels

PROBABLE SCENARIO

My ex discussing
ecclesiastic law with the Pope
while they sip dry red wine
and eat prosciutto and
portebello mushrooms
In the meantime, she
remembers to speak
to him about moving
St Francis of Assisi
into a more prominent
position since he looks
out of place parked
behind the flowers
in the outer foyer

The Pope gives her
a benign smile which
she returns in kind
and tells her it takes
centuries to decide
the smallest detail
but for her anything's
possible, picking
up the phone
he orders it be done

In the afternoon
she returns from
her little walk
in the fields
near Muenster

gathering dead weeds,
ancient stones
A wreath of white
bent-winged birds
circle overhead

GOD'S BREAKFAST FOOD

Let out in the garden to peck at grasshoppers
that have come to strip the greenery
the chickens wandering in the raspberries
and along the rows of bush beans
start exploding in spontaneous combustion
as if the sun was spilling a little gasoline
on each plump white feathery duster
before God strikes a wooden Eddy's match
on the seat of his shiny pants

They bob and weave among zucchini leaves
looking down at the immediate earth
in front of their beady little bug eyes
Jaunty red combs and shaking wattles
give them a devil-may-care look
as each in turn goes poof up in flames
only the legs and the beaks escape immolation
and the perfectly cooked soft-boiled eggs
I find here and there on the weedy ground

INTO THE FOREST

Fields covered
with white geese
walking over
barley swathes
Fox running
back and forth
trying to pick out
a dinner companion
Beaten down
by thrusting wings
finally grabs a neck
bends it to the ground

Trying to think
of a few words
to explain why geese
stood around gabbling
rather than flying
away from danger
I forget why,
the moment escaped
Eyes of the universe
watching every move
as if predetermined

From the order of chaos
a new master drags
winged victory
into the forest
A few loosened feathers
a little light along
the bottom of the clouds

MEDITATION ON A BIRD'S SKULL

How soon the summer goes awry,
blackbirds turning into black clouds
in the clear crisp fall air
flit around the harvest sun
moving in unison, one entity
rises and falls in a modest breeze
flying south for a new season

First frost lightly in the grass
burns fiery against falling leaves
Greater Canada geese fuelling up
in grain-spilled fields stagger about
easily mistaken from a distance
for old men wearing black
and grey raincoats leaving the bar
at Bladworth or Craik

I see them along the roadside
taking a leak in the dusty margins
all that grain flowing from the beer
back into the prairie earth
watering the sparse yellow flowers
that lift their ruined heads
into the wind and die slowly forever

MEETING THE APOSTLES ON THE ROAD TO HEAVEN

The poets are here,
walking past the hedges
on the hard-packed roadway
Passing the paper cornfield
on their way back from the cemetery
I can hear their feet crunch
on the gravel and the hesitant
nervous gasoline laughter
poured onto the words
before they stop
and light the match
Not in grace I pass by

Small grey birds the monks
have taught to walk
on their arms and shoulders
for a thousand generations
flutter down from spruce branches
and hover over tiny snow-
flake crumbs melting
in my palms

Suddenly
after a great silence
the sky blows up
in my face

123

THE GRAVE

Pity the man without faith
half-starved, brutalized
digging his own grave
in wasted ground
while joking soldiers
passing a bottle
of whiskey around
stamp their feet
impatiently

If he was home
he'd make a pot of soup
and climb into his cozy bed
When he hits hard pan
the sound of the shovel
scraping the earth stops

Cold sun dancing
on his neck tickles like
a spider in the dark
Drops of sweat freeze
on lips mumbling
the shovel is my voice
Warming his hand
with his last few breaths
children's faces flash by

A single shot
echoes over the flats
A thousand white geese
feeding in the pea fields
jump, honking and gabbling
into the hole in the sky

MAGICIAN

the white rabbit
disappears in green sun-
light without trace

three shiny crows
with split tongues
drown in the dust

the amateur wives
of holy men
rest in the shade

LIKE NAPOLEON LEAVING RUSSIA

On December 5th, 1812, Napoleon
handed over supreme command to Murat.
On the night of December 18, at full gallop
the Emperor's carriage bore him through
the Arc de Triomphe and as the clock
struck the last quarter before midnight
he alighted safe and sound at the central
entrance of the Tuileries.

— J.F.C. Fuller

The sounds of thousands of horses
and men dying in the gore of Beresina
echoing in the bloody wasteland below
pungent grey clouds of cannon smoke
Frozen, broken, half-dead army stragglers
in their thousands plunging into snowy fields
Knives of death pulled hard across
the bare throats of the nearly-done-in
by the ghostly fingers of invisible mercy
The newly dying twisted in grotesque postures
Angels of God pulling out their souls
freeing them over the icy plains

Napoleon rushes ahead so he can escape
without witnessing the aftermath
After three days' march the Emperor's Guard
stand down for a day of rest while
Napoleon sleeps off his miserable mood
As always, he dreams of impossible victories
against the conquering armies of mankind
throughout the centuries, waking up refreshed
by the power and glory of his own greatness

He fires up his officers with an inspiring speech
about turning adversity into advantage
In the middle of his talk he craves an egg
but nobody has seen a chicken for months
It is a simple problem that turns him rigid
and he rages about the incompetence
that is rampant in the Grand Army
He sits down at his portable writing desk and
orders the generals make him a breakfast omelet
To make matters worse the band is too frozen up
to play his favourite marching tunes

Finally, a chicken is located but alas, it's a rooster
and the Emperor is not in the mood for coq au vin
The bird, unaware it's living on borrowed time
struts around the cooking fires showing off
its shimmering neck feathers while Bonaparte
sends dispatches to the supply office
requisitioning fresh eggs for the officers mess
He is famous for taking care of every little detail
and now it's time to depart for home
In the next few months, when he begins
recruiting a new army, he'll be philosophical
about his time spent in Russia and the four
hundred and fifty thousand French corpses
he left behind to fertilize the steppes

SIEGE

The siege engine failed dislodging
the inhabitants who have burrowed
into the mountainside
Nothing to do but wait outside
until they starve to death
Three years pass, every morning
they stand naked on the parapets
bending over in our direction

The King says we must not fail
to put them all to a fiery death
for their lack of faith in the old Gods
and their failure to fear his sword
The priest thinks the winter months,
when the rains fall and the desert blooms,
will bring a great victory
He holds fire in his hands and sees
many skeletons dancing in flames

The King who also speaks
to the Gods binds the priest in chains
and locks him in a cage
with an unfed carrion eater
Charlatan, I will believe you
unless the filthy bird of truth
puts out your lying eyes

MEDITATION ON AN EMPTY PAIL

Tonight, salmon-pink clouds
float above the horizon
and I see a chariot in the sky

The white flowers in the hedge
waste themselves, day-old
bloom turns to dross

The bitterness in evergreens
blackened along the edge
like a battlefield bathed in death

From a snag the bird of life
sings God's evening song
wind ruffles its feathers

WITNESS

In the leaden winter, forty below
dark-limbed spruce trees with hoary beards
appear ghostly in ice fog
Even the sleepers in the graveyard,
sheltered by frosted hedges,
hear the bell banging on God's door

Down the hall Brother Gerald's canary
begins its morning song of redemption
to its alienated mate, brooding for a lover
Sudden bursts of colour sadder than the wilderness
travel down the polished linoleum

The oleander, in newly opened bloom,
reflected in courtyard windows,
trembles flamingo pink and fragrant
against the drifting veil of snow
It wouldn't last two minutes on the outside

It's a good thing the monks, devotion
and obedience etched in their faces
like an occupational hazard,
are singing prayers for the living
The moment of truth is upon us,
"all the bare fields silent as eternity"

WINTER EPILOGUE

The end, the withering season foretold
Now it's come to this, hoarfrost covering the trees
Sun obscured by a snow sky before it can rise
Something scrapping like a finger against the tin roof
The monks in the glass cathedral praying to God
Their faces are the faces of mankind; peaceful,
enraptured, benign, grotesque

Outside a raven flaps along the treeline
This is the raven of darkness and light
croaking in the wilderness above lonely fields
investigating every small possibility
God put him here on the grounds of the pious
A reminder that the beak of death feasts in open
country beyond the brick walls of sanctuary

HYMN FOR THE LAST ONE LEFT ON EARTH

This is the song of emptiness when every living thing
perishes in the burnt forest, on molten rivers of stone

the bleak song of bad water and poison air
that snuffed us, unable to breathe in our beds

the victory song of nuclear power plants
black rain falling on dominate city states at war

the nautical ballad of poisoned barren seas
of cloned man-made fish swimming in pens

the death song, anthem of the prairie farmer
under the genetic-master investors on Wall Street

the whistling tune of the traveller leaving on the bus
before the boss finds the cash missing

the song without glory that asks forgiveness
for taking more than the earth had to give

the simple song of the believer who desires paradise
but feels unworthy because of all the bloodshed

This is the bitter/sweet song at the end of time when God
sets all the birds in the sky down on a branch in heaven

Notes

Time has an interesting way of arbitrating 'how' and 'why' poems stay around or are sorted out in a writing life. For a while, I was tempted to subtitle this collection: *An unnatural history of birds* since it is an energetic, poetic discourse that travels in every direction throughout the vistas of bird life. Ultimately the poems reveal the human condition and how perceptions can be suffused, altered, or even compromised by the arrival of our feathered friends. Suddenly it came to me as lightly as a feather drifting gently on a summer breeze — sometime, perhaps long in the past, I had ceased being a bird watcher and had become a bird writer. The poet in this book has been writing bird poems for over three decades. The birds that appear in the various poems have found their way into the poet's psyche by an unconscious or semi-conscious process. Birds exist in numbers in nearly every landscape but especially in the internal landscape beneath the dome of the sky. Each of the poems in this collection somehow celebrates the compelling presence and influence of birds in the universe

Essentially, this volume is my *selected and new bird poems* from a life's catalogue of mostly out of print (or yet to be printed) works. This volume contains eighty two poems: forty poems selected from eight previous small press editions and forty two new poems that have not previously been published. The first and only appearance of the five "translations" in Section One was in a limited edition printing entitled *Okira*, Blackfish Press 1976.

The author wishes to thank the Saskatchewan Writers Guild and the Saskatchewan Arts Board for various programs that have enabled the process. With thanks to Dolores Reimer for an always interesting dialogue about the text and to Pat Friesen and Joe Rosenblatt for their friendship and devotion to poetry